THE MIDDLE PASSAGE

WHITE SHIPS | BLACK CARGO

THE MIDDLE PASSAGE

WHITE SHIPS | BLACK CARGO

TOM FEELINGS

INTRODUCTION BY DR. JOHN HENRIK CLARKE

Dial Books *New York*

*To my mother, Anna, and grandmother, Julia, whose powerful love insisted that
I was balanced enough to take on this challenge. To my friend, Andaiye, from Guyana,
who chose to enter the bowels of the slave ship with me, bringing her (old people's)
wisdom and patience, strengthening me for the long, lonely passage through the middle.
And finally to my lovely wife, Dianne, and our baby daughter, Niani Sekai,
my rewards, waiting for me, on this side of the journey.*

T. F.

Published by Dial Books
A Division of Penguin Books USA Inc.
375 Hudson Street
New York, New York 10014

Copyright © 1995 by Tom Feelings
Introduction copyright © 1995 by Dr. John Henrik Clarke
Map rendering copyright © 1995 by Anita Karl/James Kemp
Map based on *The African Diaspora Map*, copyright © 1990 by Joseph E. Harris,
used by permission of Joseph E. Harris, Howard University.
All rights reserved
Editor: Phyllis J. Fogelman
Typography by Atha Tehon
Printed in Italy
First Edition
1 3 5 7 9 10 8 6 4 2

Library of Congress Cataloging in Publication Data
Feelings, Tom.
The middle passage : white ships/black cargo / Tom Feelings ;
introduction by Dr. John Henrik Clarke.
p.   cm.
Includes bibliographical references and map.
ISBN 0-8037-1804-7.—ISBN 0-8037-1965-5 (signed limited edition)
1. Feelings, Tom. 2. Africans in art. 3. Slavery and slaves in art.   I. Title.
ND237.F32A4   1995   759.13—dc20   95-13866   CIP

*The artwork was rendered using pen and ink and tempera on rice paper.
It was printed in tritone, using two black inks and one gray,
plus a neutral press varnish.*

The writer Paule Marshall once spoke of the "psychological and spiritual journey" that we must take back into the past in order to move forward. You have to engage the past, she said—to deal with it—"if you are going to shape a future that reflects you."

My personal journey started in the late 1950s, with drawing from life in my own community in the streets of Brooklyn, New York, U.S.A., drawing all the faces and places I had seen most of my life but hadn't put down on paper until that point. I eventually took those developing skills to West and East Africa, the Caribbean islands, and finally to South America, physically tracing the trail from the motherland, Africa, through and into the diaspora—those places outside of Africa where black people now live. I was taking the "journey back in order to move forward."

Though I have been drawing and painting since I was a child, it was during the early 1960s that I became the most emotionally, spiritually, and creatively involved with depicting images of my own people. The civil rights movement was sweeping America. Hundreds of thousands of black people were standing up, marching forward, refusing to be invisible. Outside of America, African and West Indian nations were fighting for independence. Since the 1954 and 1955 Supreme Court decisions that schools were to be integrated "with all deliberate speed," violence was being unleashed daily against any black people who tried to test the new law of the land. On television and in the newspapers, images

flashed across the country of black Americans assaulted, beaten for trying to register to vote; small black children harassed by white mobs outside of schools; black churches being bombed in the South; black college students trying to desegregate "white only" sections of public stores. As time passed and the civil rights battle continued to heat up, all of these images—a mixture of pride, shame, anger, and despair—started moving into both my consciousness and my art, reflecting the frustration and sorrow of that period. I became concerned about a lack of balance in my work. As a black American I knew where the sorrow and pain came from, and it was beginning to overwhelm me personally. I wanted to know where the joy I felt, down deep, came from. Where did this joy originate?

So in 1964 I moved to West Africa. Africa. The original home of all black people. The country I chose to go to was Ghana. Ghana under President Kwame Nkrumah was in the forefront of the fight for African independence and a unified Africa. President Nkrumah welcomed the skills of black people from the Americas and the Caribbean. I lived and worked there for two years as an illustrator for the Government Publishing House. And I did see the joy. Africa heightened my feelings of identity. For the first time in my life I was in the majority. I gained strength in my convictions, going out into the community of Accra, drawing all those places and faces my heart and eyes yearned to see and feel. Living in Africa reaffirmed much that was positive that I had deep inside me about black people. My drawings became more fluid and flowing. Rhythmic lines of motion, like a drumbeat, started to appear in my work, and a style that incorporated a dance consciousness surfaced. My black-and-white paintings became brighter, the contrast glaring, a luminous glowing atmosphere of warm light set against and around dark skin. Even my colors became more vivid and alive, as though they possessed a light radiating from within.

Only once in Africa did the muted monochromatic somber colors of my art from America surface in my mind. One night while speaking with a Ghanaian friend, he asked quite unexpectedly, "What happened to all of you when you were taken away from here?" I knew instantly that he meant "what happened to all our people who were forcefully taken from Africa, enslaved, and scattered throughout the 'New World'?" He was referring to all those Africans, our ancestors, viciously uprooted from their homes and taken by European slave ships on the hideous sea journey across the Atlantic Ocean. He was referring to this crossing called the Middle Passage.

As he continued to speak, muted images flashed across my mind. Pale white sailing ships like huge white birds of prey, plunging forward into mountainous rising white foaming waves of cold water, surrounding and engulfing everything. Our ancestors, hundreds of them locked in the belly of each of these ships, chained together like animals throughout the long voyage from Africa toward unknown destinations, millions dying from the awful conditions in the bowels of the filthy slave galleys.

Is this what he wanted to know? Who could tell him this story with any kind of balance? Who would want to force himself emotionally into that horrible time to tell this story and risk the loss of sanity by stepping back into what has to be the most agonizing experience for any black person alive? Yet visually, for an artist, for a storyteller, what could be more

challenging than this powerful, profound dramatic history, probing the memory, fueling the imagination, maybe even becoming a vehicle for creative growth? I began to see how important the telling of this particular story could be for Africans all over this world, many who consciously or unconsciously share this *race memory*, this painful experience of the Middle Passage. All of our ancestors, from so many different villages and regions of Africa, speaking different tongues, herded together into those miserable vessels, shared this horrible crossing of the waters.

But if this part of our history could be told in such a way that those chains of the past, those shackles that physically bound us together against our wills could, in the telling, become spiritual links that willingly bind us together now and into the future—then that painful Middle Passage could become, ironically, a positive connecting line to all of us whether living inside or outside of the continent of Africa.

I didn't answer my friend's question that night. Not in words. But unknowingly, he had started me thinking about how, in some form, I might be able one day to tell that story.

Nearly ten years would pass before this form would reveal itself to me. Within that period of time I returned to America, entering for the first time the newly integrated—one of the civil rights movement successes—world of children's book publishing as an illustrator. For five years, with my main focus on African themes, I illustrated mostly picture books that I believed reflected my joy of living in Africa and projected that continent's heritage of celebration. My books emphasized the beautiful side of that black experience, especially for black children in America, whom I knew were bombarded daily with negative texts and images of our ancient homeland.

In 1971 I was invited to the newly independent country of Guyana, the only English-speaking country in South America (formerly British Guiana, colonized by Holland and England, now populated by Africans who were imported and enslaved by the Dutch; by East Indians who were brought in by the British as indentured servants; and by Amerindians, the country's original inhabitants). This young third world republic of people of color rightly wanted to represent this majority by establishing a children's book unit within their ministry of education. I was brought in to train the local artists to illustrate texts written by the ministry's teachers. These texts and images were committed to telling the correct historical, painful truth to the children about how each group came to Guyana and who brought them there and why. A special emphasis was put on how they must now all work together to develop their new nation as free people. The project was designed to help the children *face* their history, straight on.

It was here, in this context, that I began to see that this was a form I could use. It could be a way of fulfilling my desire to show pain and sorrow as an unavoidable condition of black life, yet simultaneously to reveal the joy of that life's *rhythm* as an affirmation of the presence of life, all in a single project that used everything I had ever learned about the power of picture books. Storytelling is an ancient African oral tradition through which the values and history of a people are passed on to the young. And essentially I am a storyteller. Illustrated books are a natural extension of this African oral tradition. Telling stories through art is both an ancient and modern functional art form that enables an artist to communicate on a large scale to people young and old. I could use the form of historical narrative pictures telling a complete story to adults.

This would be my answer to that probing question posed to me by my Ghanaian friend in Africa years before.

Enthusiastically I started reading everything I could find on slavery and specifically the Middle Passage. I searched out and wrote down all of the factual incidents in sequential order, reading some personal accounts by former slave-ship captains, slave traders, and various European historians. I expected the descriptions of the horror of the slave forts and the inhuman treatment on the journey aboard the slave ships. But some of the writers' overbearing opinions, even religious rationalizations and arguments for the continuance of the slave trade made me feel, the more words I read, that I should try to tell this story with as few words as possible, if any. Callous indifference or outright brutal characterizations of Africans are embedded in the language of the Western World. It is a language so infused with direct and indirect racism that it would be difficult, if not impossible, using this language in my book, to project anything black as positive. This gave me a final reason for attempting to tell the story through art alone. I believed strongly that with a picture book any African in this world could pick up and see and feel what happened to us on those ships. I also wanted these images to have a definite point of view and the *passion* in them that reflected clearly the experience of the people who endured this agony. But I couldn't get the artwork started in South America. Finally I realized I had to be in a place that constantly reminded me of what I was working on and why I was working on it. For me, that was New York City. That's where the pain was.

I moved back to America. It took me two years and six months to finish the preliminary drawings. I didn't know when I started this project that time was the essential thing I needed to tell the story completely in pictures—the kind of time one associates with the form of a long novel. Time for me to open myself up and explore the mind not just of one single person going through this experience, but the minds of a whole people. A people who lived and still live this story with all its complex social and historical implications throughout the diaspora. A phrase began to form in my consciousness, one that I have often used to describe the creation of this story in pictures: "The pain of the present sometimes seems overwhelming, but the reasons for it are rooted in the past."

And as time went on, as painful as it was to force myself each time back into the agonizing past, it was equally as painful to come back through history, hoping for relief, only to see some of the same things in the present, in America, the richest country in the world . . . hundreds of the city's poor eating out of garbage cans; thousands of homeless people, young and old, across the country living in the streets; and tens of thousands of "middle class" people, black and white, on unemployment rolls . . . reminding me that a part of America's legacy is the killing off of most of its original inhabitants and importing against their will enslaved Africans to work the land, using the rationalization of skin color to continue it for centuries. A government that tolerated the dehumanization of human beings in its infancy and for such a long period of time is capable of tolerating it in the present. I was seeing the results of slavery, reminding me constantly why I was working on this project.

Still I felt the need for another kind of feedback. So for the first time in my life I let people—black people—come into my studio and look at the work in progress. I watched their faces as they went from drawing to drawing, turning page after page in sequence. All kinds of people, young and old. I listened as they voluntarily opened up and told me about the joyful and the sorrowful things in their lives. And I began to soak up all this information. All those stories, all those

things that as one person I could never experience in a single lifetime. Then when I was alone I let it seep slowly into all of my art. Years passed. I began to become uncomfortably aware of the fact that a lot of time had passed, and I was far from finished. In some cases I had to keep doing some paintings over and over until the mood was right . . . exactly right. Then and only then could I move on to the next one, sometimes trying to force the process by painting two at the same time. It wouldn't work. Sometimes overly tired, I'd tell myself that I needed sleep, trying to move away from the whole thing.

But in my feverish half-sleep my deceased maternal grandmother would come to me and say, "Get up, go back to it, and start over again . . . because you are not doing this just for yourself." My friends and others began to question why this project was taking so long. But I couldn't work any faster. Then one night I sat down and thought about all those artists and writers that I truly respected, like John O. Killens, Margaret Walker, Charles White, Paule Marshall, John Biggers . . . the ones who took the time, a long time, to finish their work in the only way they could . . . in their best way, even when it meant staying on the edge for long periods of time. And that calmed my fears.

It is almost twenty years later. I have finished this long "psychological and spiritual journey back in order to move forward" with the completion of the last painting of *The Middle Passage*—a story that has changed me forever. My struggle to tell this African story, to create this artwork as well as live creatively under any conditions and survive, as my ancestors did, embodies my particular heritage in this world. As the blues, jazz, and the spirituals teach, one must embrace all of life, both its pain and joy, creatively. Knowing this, I, *we,* may be disappointed, but never destroyed.

Nowhere in the annals of history has a people experienced such a long and traumatic ordeal as Africans during the Atlantic slave trade. Over the nearly four centuries of the slave trade—which continued until the end of the Civil War— millions of African men, women, and children were savagely torn from their homeland, herded onto ships, and dispersed all over the so-called New World. Although there is no way to compute exactly how many people perished, it has been estimated that between thirty and sixty million Africans were subjected to this horrendous triangular trade system and that only one third—if that—of those people survived.

The triangular trade system was so named because the ships embarked from European ports, stopped in Africa to gather the captives, after which they set out for the New World to deliver their human cargo, and then returned to the port of origin. The Middle Passage was that leg of the slave trade triangle that brought the human cargo from West Africa to North America, South America, and the Caribbean. This perilous trip was the most cruel and terrifying part of the triangular trade system, and its crippling effects are still very much with us today.

To endure the Middle Passage required great physical strength, mental toughness, and spiritual resolve. Under ideal sailing conditions the trip from Africa to the Americas could be completed in little over a month, but conditions were never ideal during the Middle Passage, and the average voyage took from five to twelve weeks.

It was not atypical to see a massive school of sharks darting in and out of the wake of the ships filled with human cargo plying the Atlantic. For miles they followed the battered and moldy vessels, waiting to attack the disease-ravaged black bodies that were periodically tossed into the ocean. Except for mutiny, death was the only liberation these tormented souls— Ashantis, Mandingoes, Ibos, Fulanis, Wolofs, Coromantees, and others—could expect from the stifling, fetid hold of the ship, where they had been crammed for more than a month, and where the menace of smallpox was especially fearsome.

Pinioned in the stench between the ship's decks, shackled two by two, the right wrist and ankle of one to the left wrist and ankle of another, the African captives struggled to breathe, struggled to find comfort on rough boards that tore at their naked bodies with each lurch of the ship.[1] The captives' cries of grief erupted in several different tongues; their moans and wails a common chorus of misery and hopelessness. They were human ballast, abducted from family and friends, severed from a communal life that throbbed with compassion and possibility. The agony was so relentless, their deprivation so deep and terrible, that even the sky became a faded memory.

Amid their fear and anxiety they must have wondered if they would ever see a palm tree again, ever taste once more its sweet sap and brush against its silky leaves. Would they ever hear the thunder of Africa and stand in the warm and gentle rains that nourished their crops? Would they know again what it felt like to run in fields overgrown with elephant grass, where golden calabashes glistened in the sun near the shrine of Obatala?

In the dank, crowded hold, which was about five feet high, the captives were confined in a prone position, occupying no more space than a coffin. On the larger slave ships this limited space was further constricted by a horizontal shelf or platform in the middle of it, making it possible for a second row of captives to be shelved. This practice was particularly evident on vessels captained by the dreaded "tight packers," those slavers who chose to compensate for their anticipated losses by hauling more human cargo than specified by regulations based on the size of the ship. That is, if a ship were restricted to carrying three hundred captives and the shipping company's contract called for two hundred and fifty, the captain would pack three hundred and fifty people on board to make up for those who would likely succumb to sickness or be killed during an uprising.

On the other hand, the captains who were "loose packers" believed that by giving the Africans a little more room, with better food and a limited amount of exercise and liberty, they would reduce the mortality rate and thereby command a better price for the captives at the end of the voyage. However, because the profits from the slave trade were so great, most of the slavers during the eighteenth century were tight packers.

John Newton, himself a slave-ship captain, witnessed this nefarious practice and reported on the captives' cramped quarters and the heavy leg irons that linked them together: "Every morning, perhaps, more instances than one are found of the living and the dead fastened together."[2] After

several voyages Newton quit the slave trade, became a minister, and wrote the hymn "Amazing Grace," with its autobiographical line " . . . that saved a wretch like me."

Many of the Africans huddled in the darkness cursed their fate, while others prayed and shrieked in horror each time the hatch cover closed above, virtually entombing them.[3] They had no idea what to expect; what cruel injustices still remained on the captors' list of degradation. Having been stripped from their homeland, from their gods, they could only guess what bitter misfortune awaited them. Were they to be eaten or sacrificed to the gods of their captors? The weaker ones in the hold begged their chain-mates to kill them while they slept. Others slipped into severe melancholy and trances, while others simply went mad. Even for those who survived the lice, fleas, and vicious rats, there were still the violent crews waiting topside to torture the men and to rape the women. The Middle Passage, the second leg of the Atlantic slave trade, was a horrendous experience, and death followed the ships like the wind.

The manacled and terrified Africans knew very little about the process in which they had been ensnared. While there were those among them who had experienced slavery in Africa, they were not prepared for this new form of captivity that dehumanized them and carted them away from their cherished homeland. Slavery in Africa before the arrival of the Europeans was comparatively benign; it was more akin to indentured servitude, where slaves sometimes even rose to positions of influence. In this respect it can be likened to the slavery of Ancient Greece and Ancient Rome. The Africans knew nothing of the enforced chattel slavery of the invaders. Nor did they know who they were or from whence they came.

Among the European invaders, the Portuguese led the way, although their explorations came eight hundred years after the Arab slave trade began across the Sahara Desert and which later occurred with increased frequency along the coast of East Africa. For years the Portuguese mariners had heard stories about the great riches of Africa, and they began to trade with the African countries as early as 1434. During these early trading expeditions along the coast of West Africa the Portuguese were mainly interested in gold. But soon they envisioned in the African people reserves of cheap labor. Black humanity was suddenly more precious than gold. By 1482 the Portuguese had erected the fortress of Elmina Castle on the West Coast of Africa, near present-day Takoradi, Ghana, in order to stabilize the process of capture and detention of slaves.

The Portuguese were followed by the Spanish entry into the slave trade. Yet even though slaves were taken in large numbers to Spain's New World settlements, the Spanish did not have a prominent role in the trade itself. Toward the end of the fifteenth century the English and the French entered the slave traffic. However, the first real challenge to the Portuguese was the relatively late Dutch involvement. The Dutch were ruthless in their attempts to catch up, and in twenty years they established a monopoly in the West African slave trade. This lead was not threatened until the middle of the seventeenth century, when the English and French intensified their activities. The Portuguese, Dutch, French, and English continued their participation in slaving on the West Coast of Africa until well into the nineteenth century, and even during the Civil War. And many of these captives were delivered to merchants in the United States.[4]

To facilitate the capture of Africans, the Europeans devised a method of divide and conquer, pitting one African village against the other, and then taking the spoils for themselves. The Africans were soon confronted with a dilemma: either capture or be captured. To reject the guns offered by the invaders in exchange for other Africans often proved detrimental to a village because those same guns could end up in the hands of a traditional enemy, giving them a military advantage.

The Europeans did not go to Africa bearing civilization or to uplift the people they defined as savages; their purpose was to pillage and plunder. Poor Europeans involved in the slave trade quickly prospered, improved their status, and acquired an undreamed-of wealth. By enslaving millions of Africans to labor on the plantations in the Americas, the Europeans dramatically rescued and reshaped the economies of their own destitute countries.

The Africans could not combat this European desire for conquest. They came from societies where nature was kind, furnishing them with enough food, enough land. Their societies were governed by honor and obligation, and land was neither bought nor sold.[5]

In contrast, the European temperament was shaped in part by a thousand-year-old feudal system, which was a form of slavery. Europeans came from societies where nature was stingy; where brother competed against brother for his breakfast, land, and women. Europe was just emerging from the Middle Ages, a time when poverty and disease were rampant, "an age haunted by death and damnation."[6] The Africans had never dealt with such a fiercely competitive people, a people set on asserting its dominance at any cost.

With the establishment of numerous small forts or large castles along the West African coast, the slave trade operated smoothly for the Europeans. Without the erection of these terminals—which were often under the control of Europeans recently freed from prison dungeons and given a new lease on life—the slave trade would have been a haphazard operation. The forts and castles made it possible for the captives to be conveniently warehoused until ships arrived to transport them across the sea. Of the numerous coastal slave forts, most were located in present-day Ghana, a place the Portuguese called the Gold Coast, and which eventually became the hub of the European slave trade. If a sufficient supply of captives were not available at a designated fort, it was possible to meet a contract by procuring them from others nearby. Another prominent fort located on Gorée Island, off the coast of Senegal, was a central point controlled by the French.

The misery the captured people experienced in these forts or castles was exceeded only by the horrific conditions in the holds of slave vessels. To some degree, for thousands of Africans these dungeons were harbingers of the tragedy ahead. The captives were as tightly packed in the forts as they would be in the ships; at times during the early years of the trade there were as many as three hundred to five hundred captives imprisoned in a fort. And for the unruly captives who refused to obey the sting of whips, there was solitary confinement in small boxes with a hole at the top to allow the captive's head to protrude.

After the slavers exhausted the supply of villagers around the forts, they pushed inland. Millions of Africans perished during these raids on villages and on the long marches to the forts where their movements were restrained by coffles.[7] Later many more of them would die in the filthy dungeons.

Each fort had a door of no return through which captives exited, leaving their beloved homeland for the last time. By the time they were herded down through that door and onto the beach, they had begun not only a journey across an ocean of despair, but on a nightmare of African family destruction that to this day continues to have a devastating impact on the psychological and economic well-being of black Americans.

African captives found a measure of relief on the slave ships through revolts and mutinies, which were a common occurrence. One clear indication of this is the costly insurance premium the shipping companies had to pay. Lloyd's of London, one of the world's wealthiest insurance companies, was virtually launched by insuring slave ships.[8] Certainly the Africans did not accept their servitude peacefully. To deter the possibility of mutiny, the captives—particularly the men—were kept chained at all times, even during the brief periods topside when they were forced to exercise by dancing and jumping, in order to protect the slavers' investments as well as to vent mounting hostility. These exercises were often accompanied by Africans playing banjos, and beating drums or upturned kettles. Even so, the potential mutiny was an event that bothered the sleep of every captain of a slave ship.

Nor did the crew rest without fear. In fact there was little rest for them at all as they faced an endless round of duties. They were lucky to survive one voyage, and rarely made a second. The conditions of their employment forced them to deny the humanity of the Africans; and all too often they began to question the value of their own humanity.

There were successful uprisings in which the Africans gained control of the ships and were able to steer them back to their homeland. A memorable mutiny was led by Joseph Cinque in 1839. Cinque and the other rebels killed the captain and took over the slaver *Amistad*. They were eventually captured and tried for murder and piracy on the high seas.

However, in the end they were acquitted of all charges.[9] Other revolts resulted in the loss of crew members as well as captives. Those who could not mutiny resorted to other forms of resistance. Women were often the most troublesome. They would devise ways of making constant, loud, and unnerving noises that would drive the crew to distraction. And of course there were many who chose suicide—mainly by jumping into the shark-infested ocean—rather than allow the Europeans to determine their destiny.

But despite the miserable conditions, inadequate space and food, deadly diseases, and the violence from crew members, millions of African captives survived, demonstrating their strength and implacable will. In humankind's shameful history of forced migrations, the journey of the Africans from their bountiful homeland to the slave markets of the New World is one of the most tragic. It is a story that can never be told in all its gruesome details. Of the countless number of Africans ripped from the villages of Africa—from the Sénégal River to northern Angola—during the nearly four centuries of the slave trade, approximately one third of them died on the torturous march to the ships and one third died in the holding stations on both sides of the Atlantic or on the ships. It is estimated that ten to twenty million arrived in the New World alive, to be then committed to bondage. If the Atlantic were to dry up, it would reveal a scattered pathway of human bones, African bones marking the various routes of the Middle Passage.

But those who did survive multiplied, and have contributed to the creation of a new human society in the Americas and the Caribbean. It is a testament to the vitality and fortitude of the Africans that ten to twenty million lived through the heinous ordeal that many consider the greatest crime ever committed against a people in human history.

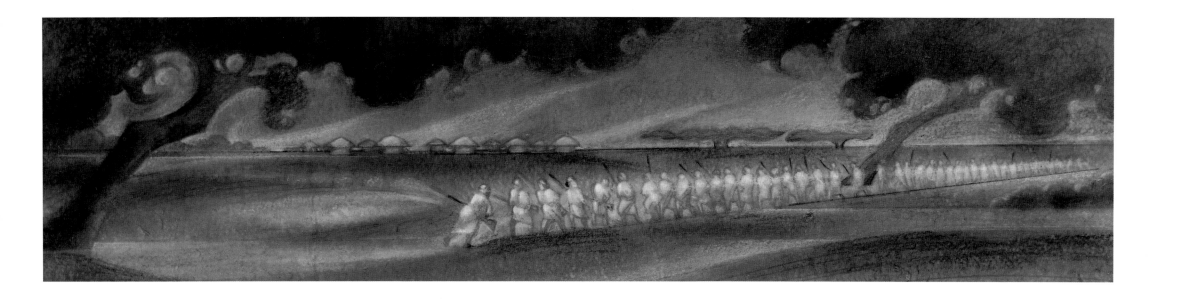

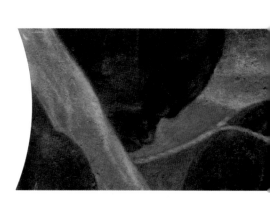

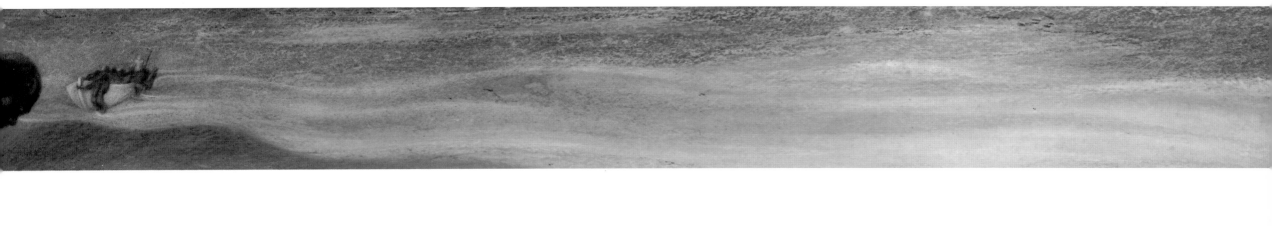

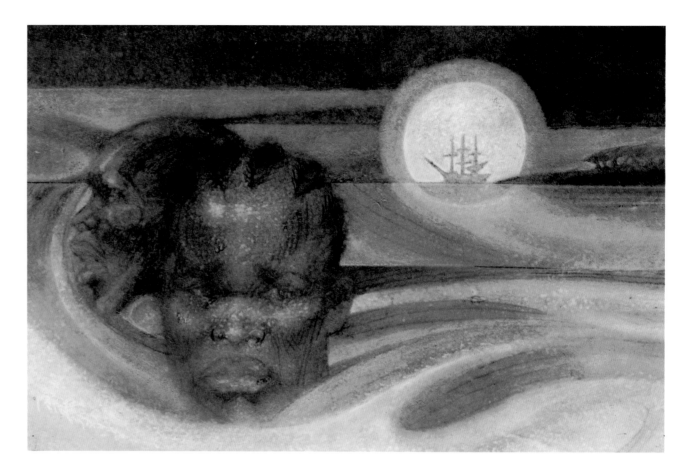

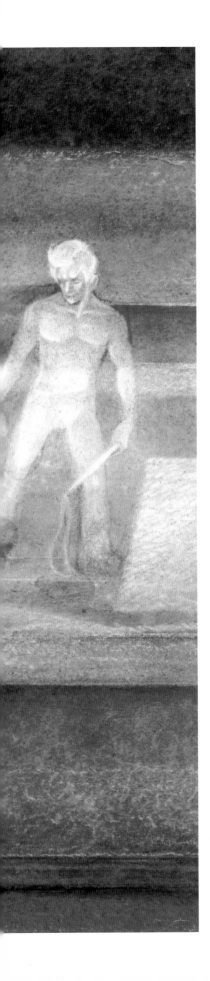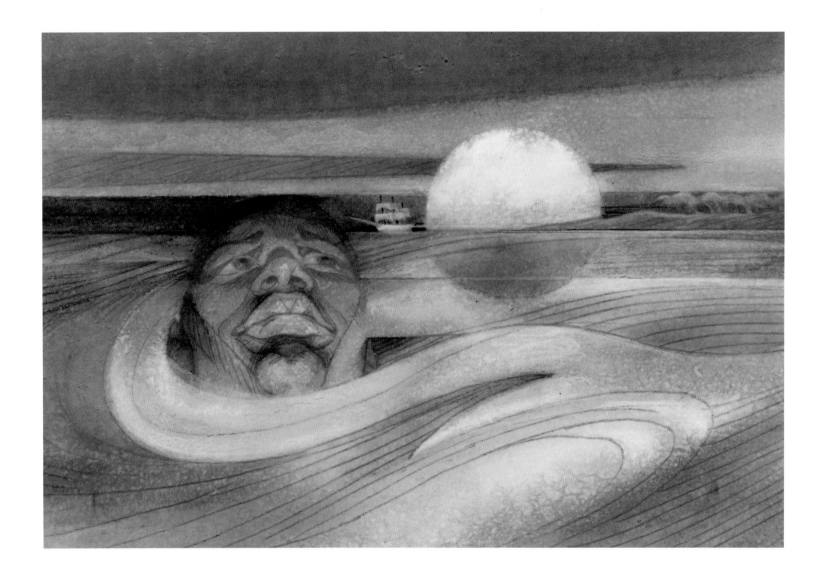

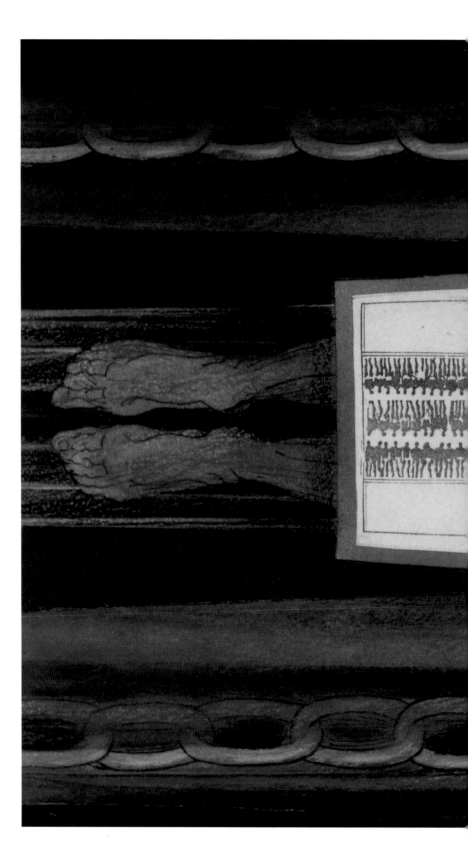

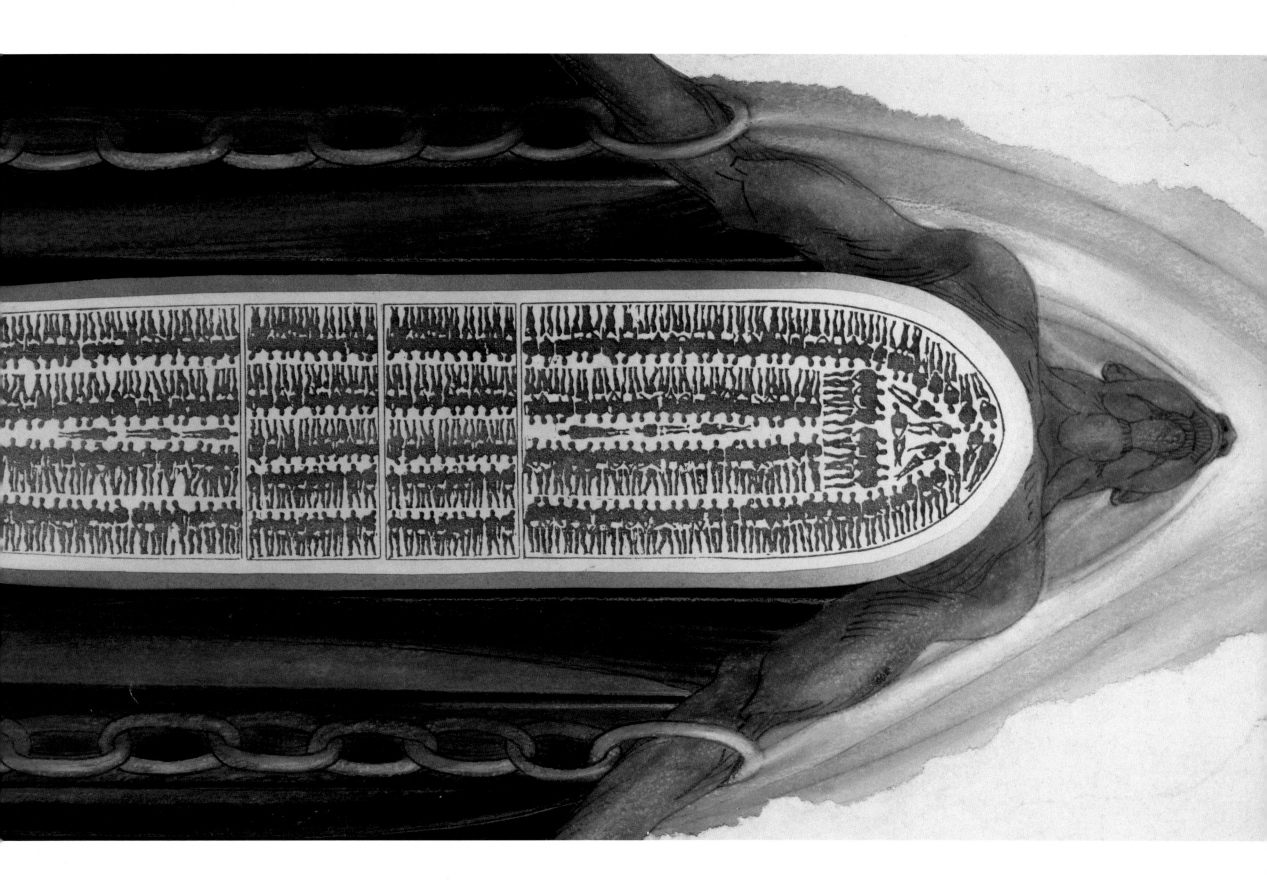

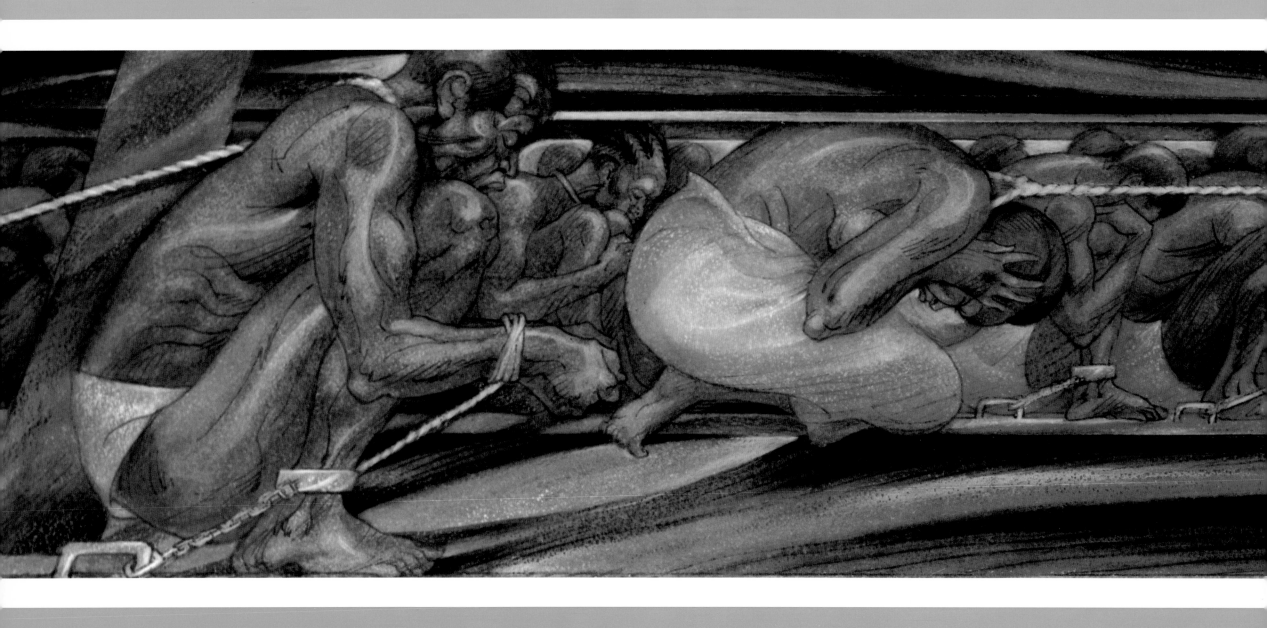

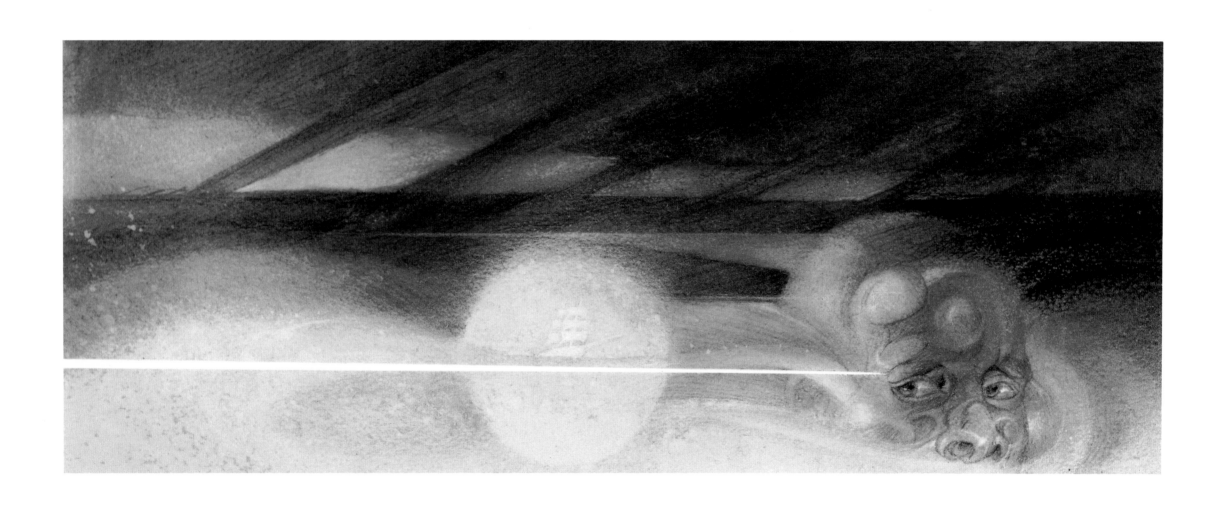

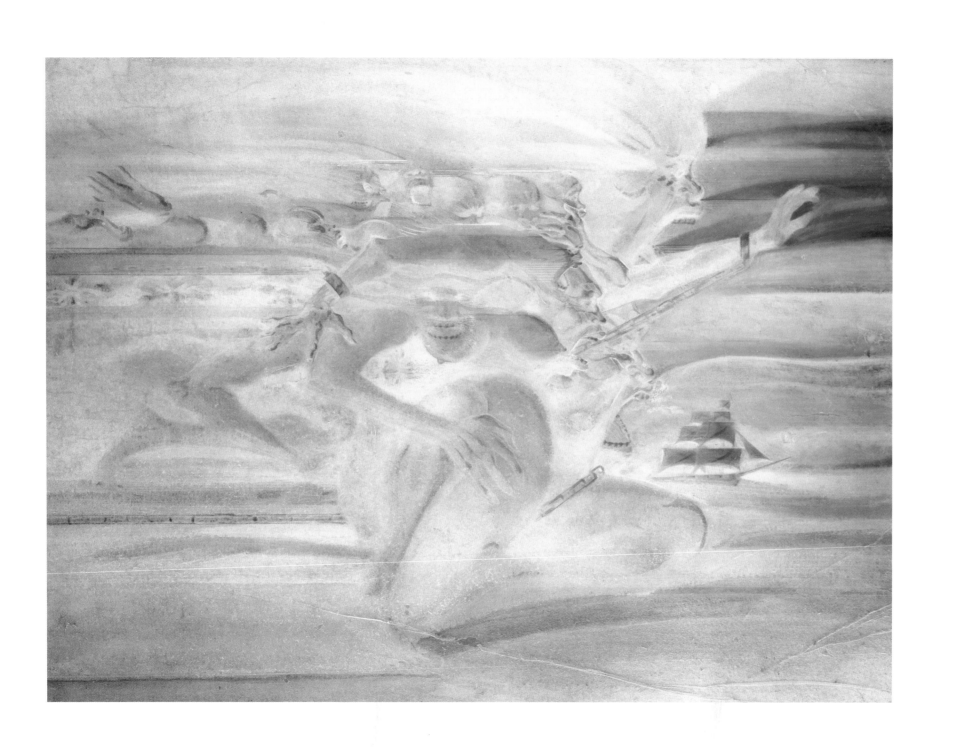

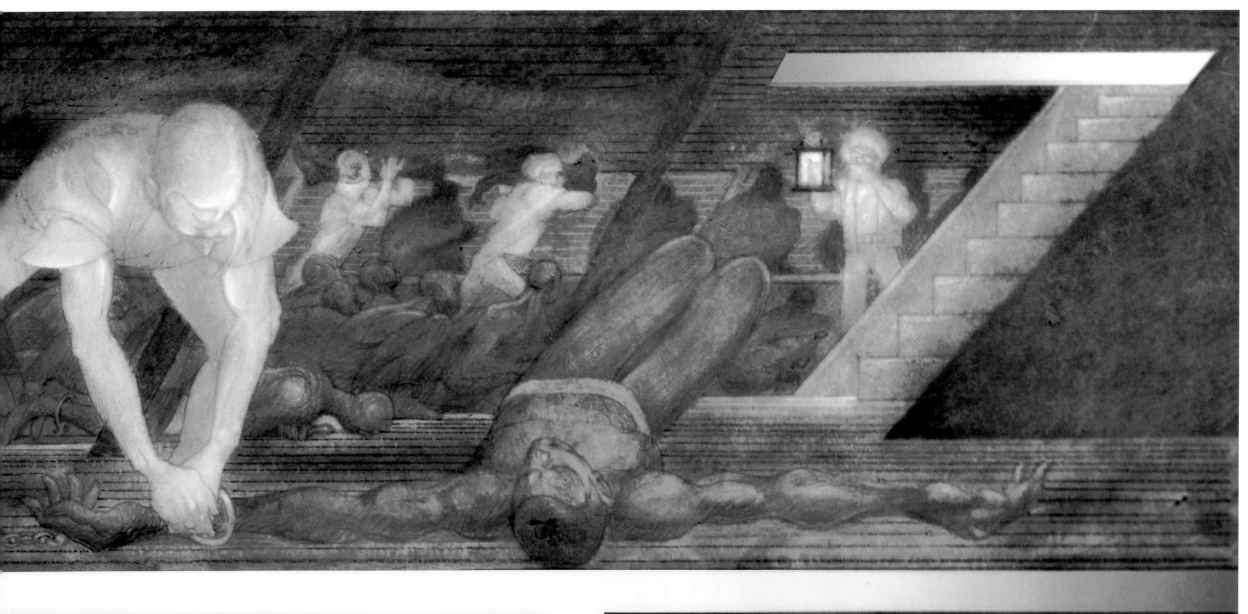
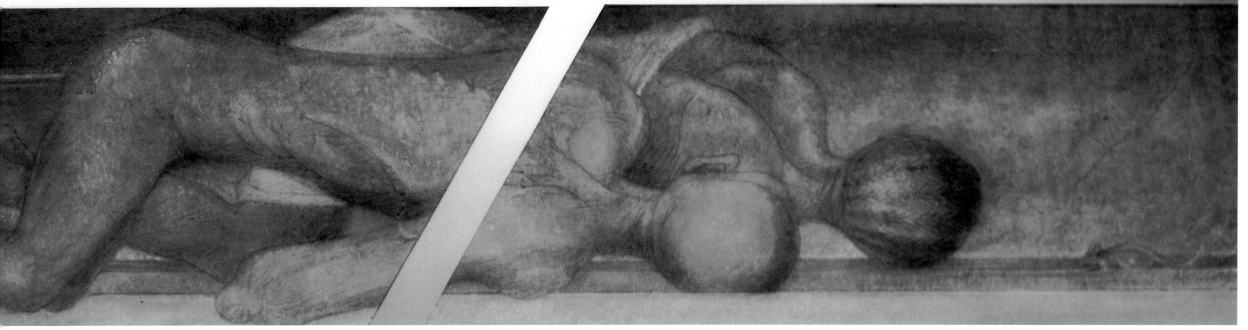

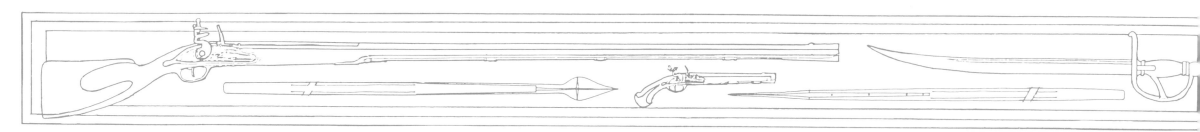

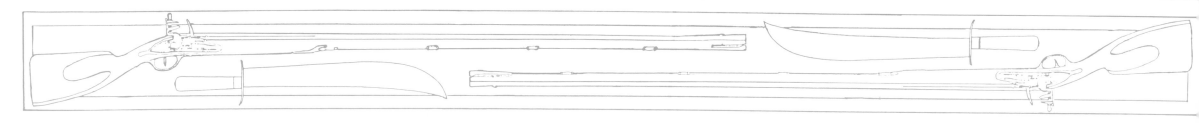

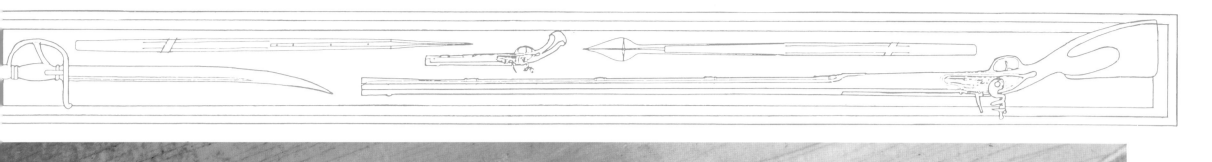

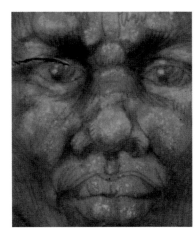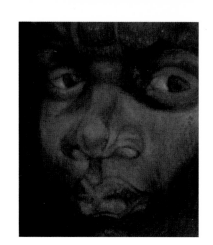

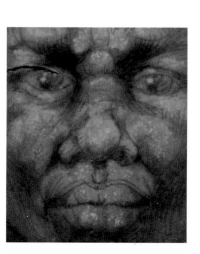

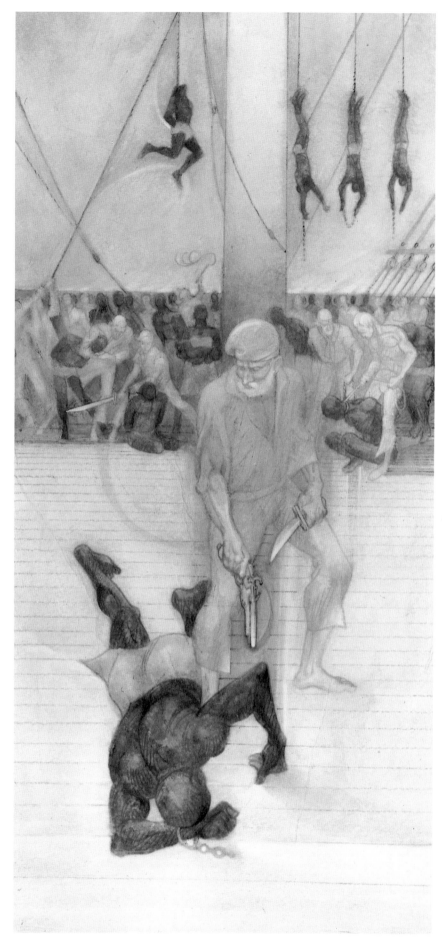

BIBLIOGRAPHY

BAYLISS, JOHN F. *Black Slave Narratives*. London: Collier Books, 1970.

CLARKE, JOHN HENRIK. *Christopher Columbus & the African Holocaust: Slavery & the Rise of European Capitalism*. Brooklyn, New York: A & B Books Publishers, 1992.

FRANKLIN, JOHN HOPE. *From Slavery to Freedom*. New York: Knopf, 1980.

KATZ, WILLIAM LOREN. *Breaking the Chains: African-American Slave Resistance*. New York: Atheneum, 1990.

MANNIX, DANIEL P. AND MALCOLM COWLEY. *Black Cargoes*. New York: Viking Press, 1962.

OLIVER, ROLAND. *The African Experience*. New York: HarperCollins, 1991.

PAIENWONSKY, ISIDOR. *Eyewitness Accounts of Slavery in the Danish West Indies*. New York: Fordham University Press, 1989.

ROBERTS, J. M. *History of the World*. London: Oxford University Press, 1993.

ROGERS, J. A. *World's Great Men of Color*, Vol. I. New York: Collier, 1946.

WILLIAMS, ERIC. *Capitalism and Slavery*. Chapel Hill: University of North Carolina Press, 1944.

———. *From Columbus to Castro: The History of the Caribbean 1492–1969*. New York: Vintage, 1970.

FOOTNOTES

[1] Daniel P. Mannix and Malcolm Cowley, *Black Cargoes* (New York: Viking Press, 1962), p. 105.

[2] Mannix and Cowley, *Black Cargoes,* p. 106.

[3] Isidor Paienwonsky, *Eyewitness Accounts of Slavery in the Danish West Indies* (New York: Fordham University Press, 1989), p. 53.

[4] Mannix and Cowley, *Black Cargoes*, pp. 284-85.

[5] J. A. Rogers, *World's Great Men of Color,* Vol. I (New York: Collier, 1946), p. 247.

[6] J. M. Roberts, *History of the World* (London: Oxford University Press, 1993), p. 413.

[7] Roland Oliver, *The African Experience* (New York: HarperCollins, 1991), p. 125.

[8] Eric Williams, *Capitalism and Slavery* (Chapel Hill: University of North Carolina Press, 1944), p. 52.

[9] William Loren Katz, *Breaking the Chains: African-American Slave Resistance* (New York: Atheneum, 1990), p. 121.

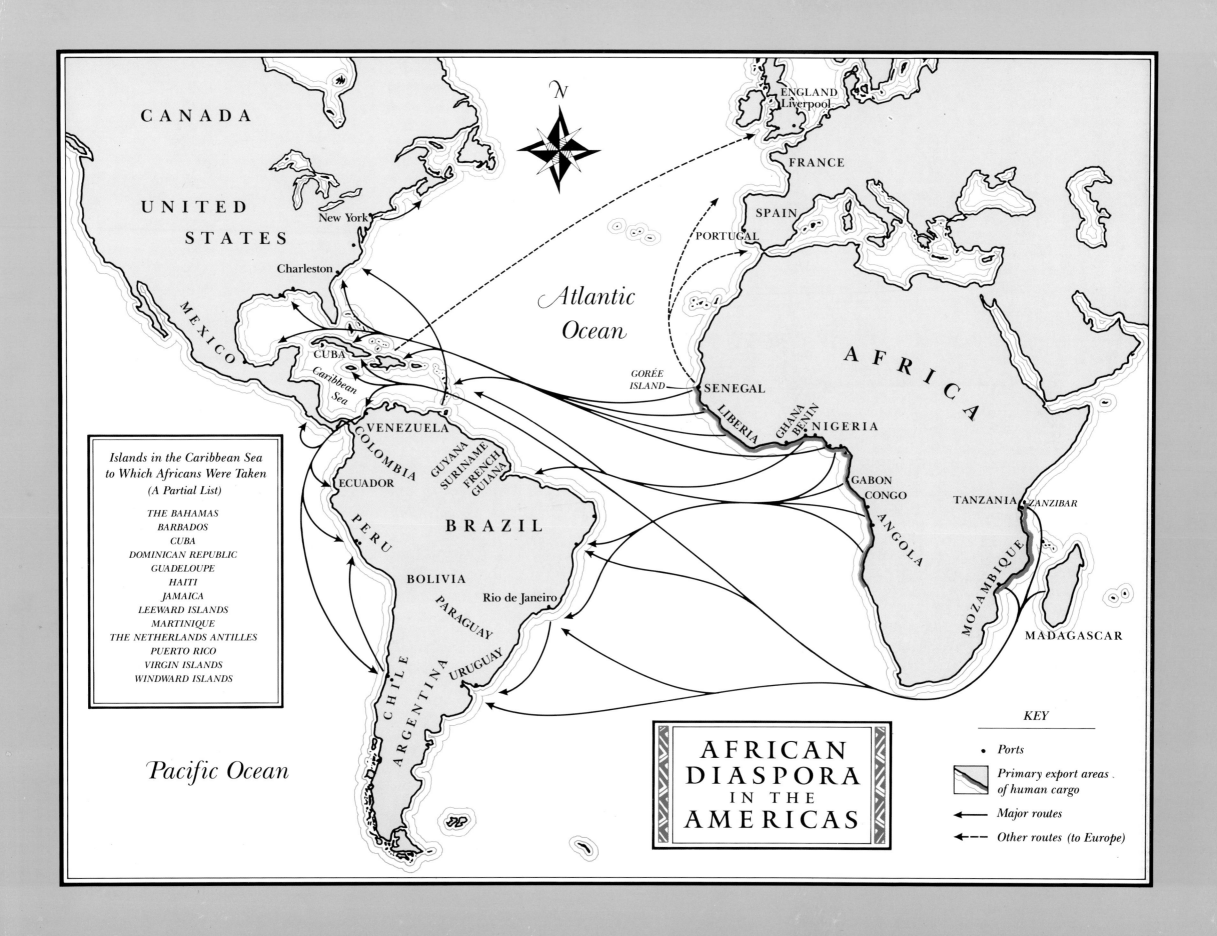

CANADA

UNITED
STATES

New York

Charleston

MEXICO

CUBA

Caribbean
Sea

VENEZUELA

COLOMBIA

ECUADOR

GUYANA
SURINAME
FRENCH
GUIANA

PERU

BRAZIL

BOLIVIA

Rio de Janeiro

PARAGUAY

URUGUAY

CHILE

ARGENTINA

Pacific Ocean

*Atlantic
Ocean*

ENGLAND
Liverpool

FRANCE

SPAIN

PORTUGAL

GORÉE
ISLAND

SENEGAL

LIBERIA

GHANA
BENIN

NIGERIA

AFRICA

GABON
CONGO

ANGOLA

TANZANIA ZANZIBAR

MOZAMBIQUE

MADAGASCAR

*Islands in the Caribbean Sea
to Which Africans Were Taken
(A Partial List)*

THE BAHAMAS
BARBADOS
CUBA
DOMINICAN REPUBLIC
GUADELOUPE
HAITI
JAMAICA
LEEWARD ISLANDS
MARTINIQUE
THE NETHERLANDS ANTILLES
PUERTO RICO
VIRGIN ISLANDS
WINDWARD ISLANDS

**AFRICAN
DIASPORA
IN THE
AMERICAS**

KEY

• Ports

Primary export areas
of human cargo

← Major routes

←--- Other routes (to Europe)

ACKNOWLEDGMENTS

There are so many people to acknowledge, too numerous to list, who played some part in this project directly or indirectly, whether they know it or not. People who helped set it in motion or kept it moving forward with their active encouragement, and those who waited patiently, and impatiently, for me to finish. All are important to me now. But for those who are no longer with us, who have passed on, yet whose spirits are still within me, I feel it is crucial and very important for me to name them. For to say their names, to remember them by repeating their names, is to keep them alive. I remember in my family my aunt Josephine Nash, my uncles Albert and Pollard Nash, and my father, Samuel Feelings. To my friends and mentors Elton Fax, John O. Killens, Charles White, Julian Mayfield, Ana Liva Mayfield, St. Clair Drake, George Wilson, Sara Lee, Sylvia Boone, Kofi Bailey, Alphaeus Hunton, Geri Wilson, Alice Childress, Romare Bearden, Shirley Graham DuBois, Owen Dodson, Simon Shulman, Melba Kgositsile, Don Lynn, and Dickie Robinson.

And to the living: my sons Zamani and Kamili. Trying to balance individual responsibility and collective responsibility, especially to the two of you, has been a struggle for me. I am sure too many times this struggle felt one-sided and seemed unfair because I wasn't there for you. But now, here in the present, I will take the time to build our relationships.

All this work could not have been published without some very important people working in the background. I thank my agent, Marie Brown, for doing what she does so well. Dr. John Henrik Clarke for bringing his volume of brilliant scholarship to the Introduction. And a special thanks for the talented touch of wordsmith Herb Boyd. And of course I thank my editor and publisher of over twenty-five years, Phyllis Fogelman, who has done more than her share of waiting for the completion of the artwork, and who has worked diligently and harmoniously with her art director, Atha Tehon, to produce a beautiful book. I thank you both again.

Finally, to all those wonderful ordinary, extraordinary people who have touched my life, from America to Africa, from Ghana to Guyana. Especially those of you who saw these images in progress and sometimes with your eyes, sometimes with your words, helped me to give this story back, in this form. I hope you all understand that your spirit lives within this book in the most positive way, even if your name is not listed here.

NKONSONKONSON
We are linked in both life and death. Those who share common blood relations never break apart.